C000125560

NENE VALLEY RAILWAY
A JOURNEY BY STEAM
by Nathan Wilson

Un-rebuilt Bulleid Pacific no.34081 92 SQUADRON, a member of the Battle of Britain Class locomotive that served the southern railways of England prepares to move off shed ahead of its duties past its Eastern Region counterpart – Peppercorn A1 pacific no.60163 TORNADO. *Martin Vos*

Published by Mainline & Maritime Ltd, 3 Broadleaze, Upper Seagry, near Chippenham, SN15 5EY
Tel: 01275 845012
www.mainlineandmaritime.co.uk   orders@mainlineandmaritime.co.uk
Printed in the UK

ISBN: 978-1-900340-68-7   © Mainline & Maritime Ltd & Contributors 2020
All rights reserved. No part of this publication may be reproduced by any process without the prior written permission of the publisher.
Cover images are reproduced and captioned in the text.

INTRODUCTION

The Nene Valley Railway has played a role throughout my life – when I was a child it was a place my Grandad, a former fireman based at New England would bring me for family days out, and as I grew older it carried on being a place I frequented with my parents and family.

An ambition of mine was to become a fireman, like my Grandad, and in late summer of 2011 I joined as a volunteer, with my first footplate turn on THOMAS coming in the December of that year. As well as footplate duties I volunteered down in the shed, helping first with the overhaul of 92 SQUADRON before taking on the cosmetic restoration of DEREK CROUCH and forming The Small Loco Group.

In February 2014 I achieved my ambition and reached the grade of fireman, and I have been very privileged and fortunate to crew some fantastic locomotives.

The skills I learnt in the Mechanical Engineering Dept. lead me to become a Boilersmith Apprentice, firstly based at the North Norfolk Railway for twelve months in their boiler dept. completing the first year of the BESTT (Boiler Engineering Skills Training Trust) Boilersmith Apprenticeship scheme, before carrying out four months on their running maintenance side. I was then given the opportunity to move to Locomotive Maintenance Services in Loughborough in October 2016, where I spent a further two years as an apprentice, completing the entire BESTT programme and becoming their first apprentice to complete the entire course. I also gained the opportunity of working on the mainline with The A1 Steam Locomotive Trust with TORNADO making many new friends at various heritage railways across the country, and giving me experiences I will never forget.

In February 2020 my journey went full circle as I was offered a job working back at Wansford in the Mechanical Engineering Dept. as a fitter bringing the skill set I learnt across the past five years back to the railway, to pass on to volunteers and to help further the capabilities of the Dept.

Which brings me to why I've compiled this book. If it wasn't for the Nene Valley Railway giving me the many opportunities to take up roles on the footplate and in the Mechanical Engineering Dept. then I wouldn't have had any of the opportunities or experiences I have gained over the past 9 years throughout railway preservation, to complete lifelong ambitions that at one stage I could only dream about, to having met some of my best friends at the NVR, to the skills that I have learnt and been able to pass on to others, the knowledge I have gained, and the better person I have become for it. So because of everything the railway has given to me, I want to give something back to the NVR and support them when they have supported me.

I must say thank you to Oli Goodman and Martin Vos, two other NVR members and friends for their support in creating this book by allowing me to use some of their images that are found in this book, they are two extremely talented photographers and I'm delighted they agreed to support this book.

I hope you enjoy this book, looking back at some of the memorable events and locomotives to have graced the NVR over the past ten years, and please support the Nene Valley Railway to keep us steaming into the future!

Nathan Wilson

A visitor from the Severn Valley Railway was GWR Hawksworth pannier tank no. 1504. Despite being a GWR design, all ten of the 1500 class that were built were completed just after nationalisation and fell under the Western Region of British Railways. 1501 has made several visits to the NVR, running on standard services and assisting with 'Santa Specials'. Here the loco was visiting for the 2015 Steam Gala and is seen here from Wansford signal box as it approaches platform 3 to collect its next train. Coal tank no.1054's chimney can just be made out above 1501's cab, as they prepare to double head to Peterborough. *Nathan Wilson*

Here 1501 can be seen powering its way along the Castor straight, in the capable hands of Driver Adams as they head to Peterborough. *Oli Goodman*

A short term visitor in the summer of 2017 was GWR Collet 0-4-2T no.1450 from the Severn Valley Railway. The loco stayed over the summer period working NVR service trains and at Thomas weekends as well. The loco is seen here at Yarwell Junction after arrival from Wansford. *Nathan Wilson*

Here we see Collett's GWR 0-6-2T no.5619 in glorious sunshine at Yarwell Junction awaiting departure back to Wansford. 5619 was based at the NVR during the 2018 season and ran regularly throughout the year, before leaving in late 2018 for the Swindon and Cricklade Railway. *Oli Goodman*

A short term visitor in March 2020 was GWR Pannier no.4612, visiting from the Bodmin and Wenford Railway for an event commemorating the final pannier tank of this class leaving Swindon works, which saw the loco run alongside two of the class of diesel locos that were designed to replace them – the Class 14 diesel hydraulic. 4612 ran as long lost pannier 6779 over the weekend, and can be seen hear powering away from Wansford on one of the popular freight driving experiences run by the NVR Wagon Group. *Nathan Wilson*

4612 makes a glorious sight heading towards Peterborough at Castor with the freight train in the late afternoon sun.
Oli Goodman

4612 works its way over Splash Dyke with the freight train, looking the part of a typical branch line freight. *Oli Goodman*

One of the oldest locomotives to visit the Nene Valley was the Webb designed LNWR Coal Tank no.1054, which was built at the LNWR Crewe Works in 1888. It was the 250th member of its class to be built out of a total of 300, and is the sole member of its class in preservation. 1054 visited for the NVR Steam Gala in 2015, and can be seen here running round its train at Orton Mere station. *Nathan Wilson*

1054 departs Orton Mere with a local train service to Wansford, as Fireman Fincham prepares to collect the staff so they can proceed to Wansford. *Nathan Wilson*

An LNWR loco, in front of an LNWR station building! 1054 awaits its departure to Peterborough in front of the Victorian built station building. *Nathan Wilson*

Winter 2019 saw the visit of Black 5 no.44871 to assist with 'Santa Specials' and NVR service trains. The loco also worked one of the popular freight driving experiences, and as the sun starts to set over Wansford, Black 5 no.44871 moves off with the final freight driving experience course of the day with a full head of steam. *Nathan Wilson*

Earlier in the day, 44871 is seen opening up away from Wansford heading east to Peterborough. *Oli Goodman*

February 2014 saw a winter steam event with BR Standard 5 no.73050 CITY OF PETERBOROUGH and LMS Black 5 no. 45337 working alongside each other. The Saturday of the event saw no.45337 renumbered as classmate no.44837, to recreate the long lost loco that hauled the final BR train along the line. Here 44837 can be seen as it approaches Sutton Cross with a service for Wansford. *Nathan Wilson*

Black 5 no.45337 spent a few periods of time at the NVR from 2014-2016, proving very popular and a favourite of the crews, and can be seen here on a fine day heading towards Wansford through Castor cutting. *Oli Goodman*

In clear blue skies, no.45337 passes the signals at Sutton Cross on its way towards Wansford, looking right at home in the Nene Valley. *Oli Goodman*

Black 5 no.45337 glides into Wansford station in glorious sunshine with the service train from Peterborough, recreating scenes of a bygone age. *Oli Goodman*

A last minute visitor for the 2016 Steam Gala was LMS Ivatt 2MT no.46521 from the Great Central Railway. The loco had been a visitor at the North Norfolk Gala the weekend before so came in for a flying visit on its way back to home base. Here it can be seen looking just the part as it awaits the right away with a local train to Wansford. The loco made a name for itself as the star of the TV comedy series 'Oh Doctor Beeching' when it was based at the Severn Valley Railway during the 1990s. *Oli Goodman*

A former resident of the line was LMS built 4F no.44422. The loco gave good service over the years it was based at the NVR and was extremely popular with the crews, as well as being a prototypical loco for the line. Here 44422 can be seen heading past Sutton Cross on its way to Peterborough. *Oli Goodman*

Above: A Great Central resident that made a couple of visits to the NVR was LMS 3F 'Jinty' no.47406. These locos were often seen on shunting, passenger and goods workings or empty stock movements, and could be found all across the LMS network. Here we see no.47406 accelerate away from Wharf Road crossing just to the west of Peterborough with a service bound for Wansford. *Oli Goodman*

Right: During 2018, Jinty no.47406 made a short visit back to NVR to cover the railway's steam services. Here the loco is running around at Yarwell Junction, with blue skies and the autumnal colours starting to show on the trees that line the valley to Yarwell, looking along the fireman's side of the loco. *Nathan Wilson*

Completing the country branch line look, the Jinty makes its way west through the Nene Valley countryside. *Nathan Wilson*

In 2017, Jinty no.47406 made its first visit to the railway for the railway's Small Loco Fest. The Friday before the event saw the loco run a full day's photo charter with the freight set along the length of the line. Here no.47406 is seen on one of the first runs of the day crossing a damp Wansford river bridge, as a narrow boat passes underneath. *Nathan Wilson*

As the goods train approaches Sutton Cross, Driver Jennings opens up no.47406 as they make their way hurriedly back towards Wansford, passing the signals for the TPO apparatus. *Nathan Wilson*

The sun starts to break through as the Jinty works away from the river west of Ferry Meadows, climbing the incline up towards Mill Lane Bridge. *Nathan Wilson*

With brightening skies, no.47406 steams its way west along the Castor straight with the goods train in tow. *Nathan Wilson*

One of the traditional shots at Wansford is departing past the signal box, which is seen here as no.47406 works hard away past the box. It was a very damp morning as can be seen with the moisture coming off of the wagons! *Nathan Wilson*

Here no.47406 is seen shortly after arrival at Yarwell with a passenger service from Wansford. A powerful loco that was a pleasure to fire and drive. *Nathan Wilson*

On the final day of Small Loco Fest in 2017, the final service to Yarwell evolved from a double header into a triple header! Visiting Jinty no.47406, carrying 'The Small Loco Group' headboard leads Hunslet Austerity no.75008 SWIFTSURE and Hudswell Clarke no.1800 THOMAS at Yarwell Station. Here the Jinty and SWIFTSURE ran round to the east end to lead the train to Peterborough. At Wansford, THOMAS was uncoupled and banked the train out over the River Nene. *Nathan Wilson*

At Small Loco Fest, Wansford yard was turned into a freight marshalling yard. Here Jinty no.47406 shunts back down the yard while Hudswell Clarke no.1800 awaits its next turn of duty marshalling the next set of wagons. *Nathan Wilson*

In 2017, the NVR celebrated its 40th anniversary of running the line since the first train ran in 1977. For the event, LMS 4-6-0 no.46100 ROYAL SCOT attended and took part in a three day gala event. Here ROYAL SCOT is seen opening up as the train clears the cross over at the east end of Wansford River Bridge and heads east to Peterborough. *Martin Vos*

Two of the stars of the 40th Anniversary Gala, no.46100 ROYAL SCOT stands next to Deltic no.55022 ROYAL SCOTS GREY in Wansford yard. The NVR was the Deltic's first home in preservation during the 1980s. *Nathan Wilson*

With blue skies and the river bridge packed with onlookers, no.46100 ROYAL SCOT rolls up to the bracket signal in preparation for backing down onto its next Peterborough bound train. *Martin Vos*

N2 no.1744 is seen hurrying towards Wansford tunnel with a service from Yarwell. The N2s were designed for London suburban workings out of Kings Cross, and were designed for fast acceleration away from stations to keep to the tight timings. They also carried condensing gear allowing them to work on the Metropolitan lines between Kings Cross and Moorgate. *Nathan Wilson*

Two eastern locos that starred in September 2015 were Peppercorn A1 pacific no.60163 TORNADO and Gresley N2 no.1744. The two locos ran side by side over the course of the weekend, culminating both days with a double headed service. Here the N2 is seen on shed as the A1 returns to join its shed mate. *Nathan Wilson*

Another popular and regular visitor is Peppercorn A1 pacific no.60163 TORNADO. This loco is the only member of its class left – yet it isn't a survivor from BR Days. In 1990 a group of enthusiasts came together and raised the idea of a new build steam locomotive. After the drawings for an A1 were discovered in a skip in York, the plans were put in place and in 2008 TORNADO steamed into life at Hopetown Works in Darlington. As darkness falls and the loco's headlamps are lit, TORNADO simmers in Wansford station at the head of a freight set. *Nathan Wilson*

TORNADO stands purposefully and awaits its next move, to return the freight train back to Wansford at the end of a photographic charter, a long but well worthwhile day! *Nathan Wilson*

In January 2019 TORNADO ran a photo charter along the Nene Valley recreating a BR Mixed freight from days gone by. Here the loco is seen drifting out of the western portal of Wansford Tunnel, carrying the BR Express Freight head code. The loco and wagons looked superb together. *Nathan Wilson*

As the winter sun fades, TORNADO storms across Lynch River Bridge heading towards Wansford with the freight train in tow. A sight that hasn't been seen since the 1960s – An A1 hauling a BR freight train. *Nathan Wilson*

Two East Coast giants meet at Orton Mere, as A1 no.60163 TORNADO awaits A3 no.60103 FLYING SCOTSMAN to clear the single line section between Orton Mere and Peterborough. *Nathan Wilson*

At the railway's 'Best of British event' in April 2016, Peppercorn A1 no.60163 TORNADO was the star attraction, and can be seen running towards Castor crossing in full flight. *Nathan Wilson*

After a long day's running, A1 no.60163, sporting its BR Brunswick Green livery basks in the setting sunlight as it backs into Wansford yard. *Oli Goodman*

At the 2014 Steam Gala, and sporting the very popular BR Express Passenger Blue livery, A1 no.60163 TORNADO sits on Wansford shed waiting the next turn of duty. *Nathan Wilson*

After TORNADO's first visit in March 2012, it has been a regular visitor to the NVR, and is seen here in 2012 heading a service away from Wansford and over the river Nene. *Oli Goodman*

TORNADO stands at Wansford showing its work stained look, with headlamps glowing and wagons looming out of the darkness. The photo charter was extremely popular and everybody left after having an enjoyable day! *Nathan Wilson*

A privileged view to have – looking along the fireman's side of A3 no.60103 FLYING SCOTSMAN as the loco prepares to run round its train at Wansford in preparation for heading the next service to Peterborough. *Nathan Wilson*

East Coast giants at rest. Two icons from different eras of the East Coast Main Line, A3 no.60103 and Deltic no. 55019 ROYAL HIGHLAND FUSILIER stand head to head at Wansford, the A3 stabled after a day's running and the Deltic had arrived to take part in the railway's diesel gala a few weeks later. *Nathan Wilson*

One of Gresley's most famous locomotives, A3 no.60103 FLYING SCOTSMAN drifts across Wansford River Bridge with a service from Peterborough. The A3 visited for two running events, in the Septembers of 2018 and 2019 and proved very popular with the public who came to see the locomotive. *Martin Vos*

A3 no.60103 FLYING SCOTSMAN stands under the cover of darkness after arrival at Peterborough Nene Valley with one of the railways extremely popular 'Jolly Fisherman' fish and chip trains, which run periodically and at special events across the year. *Martin Vos*

A true icon of steam, the Gresley A4 pacific, officially the fastest class of steam locomotive in the world and instantly recognisable with their distinctive streamlined shape. John Cameron's A4 no.60009 UNION OF SOUTH AFRICA has made numerous visits to the NVR over the years, most recently in 2017 and 2018 running alongside 92 SQUADRON at a September special event. Preparing to come off shed ready for another day's work, No.9 opens up to move off past fellow eastern pacific A1 no.60163 'Tornado' looking on. *Martin Vos*

Here John Cameron's A4 no.60009 UNION OF SOUTH AFRICA stands at Wansford awaiting to depart west towards Yarwell, gleaming in the late summer sun. *Oli Goodman*

No.9 rounds the bend on approach to Wansford with a westbound service from Wansford under cloudy skies. *Martin Vos*

The unmistakeable outline of an A4's front end, UNION OF SOUTH AFRICA rests on shed at Wansford shortly after arrival from the mainline in September 2017. *Nathan Wilson*

Approaching Sutton Cross TPO, No.9 leads Bulleid pacific 92 SQUADRON under the control of Driver Goodman at the NVR 'Steam in Green' event. *Martin Vos*

A legend of the steam world, Gresley A4 no.60009 UNION OF SOUTH AFRICA sits on shed at Wansford as the sun begins to set. *Nathan Wilson*

As the sun starts to set over Wansford, no.62712 MORAYSHIRE backs onto its coaches to head the final service of the day from Wansford east along the Nene Valley to Peterborough. *Nathan Wilson*

D49 no.62712 MORAYSHIRE is seen standing at Peterborough after arrival from Wansford. The loco was the star attraction at the railway's 2015 winter steam gala. *Nathan Wilson*

The LNER D49 4-4-0 carrying BR black livery is no.62712 MORAYSHIRE, a long way from the loco's home base of the SRPS at the Bo'ness and Kinneil Railway in Scotland. It is seen sitting under the station lights at Wansford on one winter's evening in February 2015. *Oli Goodman*

The Southern Region used discs for train head codes to signify the type of train the locomotive was hauling and the route it was taking. Here 92 SQUADRON carries the head code for the 'Bournemouth Belle' – one of the express trains on the Southern Region from London Waterloo to Bournemouth. *Nathan Wilson*

It's all smiles here! Driver Goodman and Fireman Wilson appear to be in good spirits aboard 92 SQUADRON as they prepare to depart Wansford with a Nene Valley service to Peterborough.
Martin Vos

The western terminus of the Nene Valley is Yarwell Junction, which is the site of the former junction of the Peterborough to Northampton and Peterborough to Market Harborough lines. The station here was built by the NVR in 2007, where 92 SQUADRON can be seen running around its train. *Martin Vos*

The beauty of early morning signing on times to prepare a locomotive for a day's running can be rewarded with spectacular sunrises – this one was no exception as the sun comes up over Wansford and 92 SQUADRON simmers away. *Nathan Wilson*

92 SQUADRON eases off Wansford shed in the middle of a heavy snow fall ahead of the days 'Santa Special' trains – only three hours earlier there was no snow in sight! *Nathan Wilson*

Bulleid Power, as 92 SQUADRON rounds the curve at Yacht Club Crossing on the approach to Overton station with a train to Wansford. This was the locomotive's first weekend back in traffic in 2017 after a major overhaul carried out at Wansford by The Battle of Britain Locomotive Society volunteers. 'The Man of Kent' was an express service on the Southern region, from London Charing Cross – Dover. *Martin Vos*

During preparations for the Southern Steam Gala in 2019, an impromptu photo opportunity arose while shunting the locos around for FTR exams and warming fires. Here MARTELLO, REPTON, and 92 SQUADRON pose in Wansford yard sporting a variety of southern region headcodes. *Nathan Wilson*

Early 2017 saw the return to service of 92 SQUADRON after overhaul. Rebuilt Bulled pacific no.34053 SIR KEITH PARK visited from the Severn Valley Railway to mark the occasion, as well as it being 50 years since the end of Southern steam. SIR KEITH PARK also took charge of NVR services the following weekend, and is seen here coasting along the Castor straight on the approach to Sutton Cross. *Nathan Wilson*

Under threatening skies, rebuilt Bulleid pacific no.34053 SIR KEITH PARK hurries around the bend on the final approach into Wansford station, seen from the Old Great North Road looking out over the Wansford flood plains. *Nathan Wilson*

The Winter Gala of 2019 saw a Southern themed event, with 92 SQUADRON starring alongside fellow Southern Region locos Schools class no.926 REPTON visiting from the North Yorkshire Moors Railway, and Terrier class no.662 MARTELLO from Bressingham Museum in Norfolk. Here REPTON can be seen stood in the yard at Wansford shortly after arrival and awaiting an FTR (Fitness to Run) exam. *Nathan Wilson*

Undertaking freight duties, Schools no.926 REPTON can be seen on the home stretch as they round the curve on the approach back into Wansford, with the River Nene laying still in the foreground. *Martin Vos*

REPTON is seen in full flight at the 2019 Winter Gala as the train approaches Yacht Club crossing with a train from Peterborough bound for Wansford. The location is just to the east of Overton (formerly known as Ferry Meadows) station and is a popular photographic location on the line. *Martin Vos*

With the winter light fading, the impressive sight of Schools class no.926 REPTON leading un-rebuilt Bulleid pacific no.34081 92 SQUADRON past the flood plains at Wansford is seen as the pair make the final approach into Wansford station with the last service of the day. *Martin Vos*

In the days leading up to the gala, REPTON was used for driving experience courses. One of the days was an advanced course, where the participant had booked the railway for the day and carried out three return trips of the line with coaching stock, getting the chance to experience driving and firing the locomotive. REPTON is seen at the head of the train prior to departing Peterborough. *Nathan Wilson*

Under the watchful gaze of Driver Purllant, REPTON is readied for moving off shed, with 92 SQUADRON, MARTELLO and a Southern brake van helping to recreate the Southern theme. *Martin Vos*

The unique BR Class 8 locomotive, no.71000 DUKE OF GLOUCESTER was the only one of its class built, and was developed with Caprotti valve gear. The three cylinders were designed to use Caprotti valve gear due to the design being more efficient than Stephenson's or Walschaerts valve gear. Here the loco heads east and away from Wansford on one of the many popular photo charters the railway has carried out over the years. 'The Duke' visited the railway for the September steam gala in 2011 and was a huge hit with crews and passengers alike. *Oli Goodman*

No.71000 DUKE OF GLOUCESTER powers over Wansford River Bridge on a photo charter working, looking every bit the part of an express passenger locomotive. Unfortunately for 'The Duke', the loco came in to service towards the end of steam on British Railways, and during trials was deemed to be poor steaming and a heavy consumer of fuel. The loco only lasted for 8 years in service before being sent to Barry Scrapyard. Its cylinders were removed so that they could be exhibited to show the workings of Caprotti valve gear. However, the loco was saved and restored at the Great Central Railway, which involved casting and machining two new outside cylinders and making a new full set of Caprotti valve gear. During the restoration, it was discovered that the chimney was too small compared to similar sized locomotives, and the dampers allowing air to the firebed were too small compared to the drawing. With these rectified, as well as some other modifications, 'The Duke' was transformed and is now recognised as one of the most powerful express steam locomotives in the UK.

Oli Goodman

During the 2011 Steam Gala, Standard 5 no.73050 CITY OF PETERBOROUGH and BR Standard Class 8 no.71000 DUKE OF GLOUCESTER worked a double headed service together. Here the pair are seen running eastbound along the Castor straight
Martin Vos

Seen through the open doors of a diesel shunter, the iconic locomotive number associated to the Nene Valley is that of BR Standard 5MT no.73050 CITY OF PETERBOROUGH, bought from British Railways by the Rev. Richard Paten with the intention of plinthing the loco outside the city's technical college. Once the loco arrived at New England shed after arriving from Manchester under its own steam, the condition of the locomotive was deemed too good to be stuffed and mounted, and as the saying goes – the rest is history. *Nathan Wilson*

Standard 5 no.73050 CITY OF PETERBOROUGH is seen here approaching Castor Mill Lane bridge, in the safe hands of Driver Watson heading towards Lynch River Bridge with a Peterborough bound NVR service train. *Nathan Wilson*

With clear skies and over a peaceful river, 73050 CITY OF PETERBOROUGH departs Wansford for Peterborough.
Oli Goodman

Another visitor from the GCR was BR Standard 2MT no.78018. This loco made itself right at home on the line and did exactly what was asked of it. Proving popular amongst the crews, here no.78018 is seen heading west along the Castor straight. *Nathan Wilson*

During the late winter months, the setting sun is just in the right position to produce shots like this – the stunning sunset captures Standard 2MT no.78018 crossing the Nene at Lynch Bridge, just to the west of Ferry Meadows. *Oli Goodman*

Standard 2MT no.78018 is seen powering away from Lynch River bridge up towards Castor Mill lane in the mid-afternoon winters sun in the Nene Valley. *Oli Goodman*

This behemoth of a tank engine, no.5485, originates from Poland, and was designed for industrial use hauling 2000 ton freight trains. With very small wheels and large cylinders, this loco is all about power over speed. The loco returned to the NVR in summer 2019 after it had been away for overhaul, which included the building of a brand new superheated boiler to replace the old one that was beyond repair. The new boiler is the first superheated standard gauge boiler to be built in the UK since the 1960s. Here the loco can be seen at Peterborough ahead of departure back to Wansford on a loaded test run during the running in period. *Nathan Wilson*

Two of the stars at the 2014 steam gala – S160 no.6046 (visiting from the Churnet Valley Railway) and A1 Pacific no.60163 TORNADO face each other as they await their next turn of duty. *Nathan Wilson*

USA 2-8-0 S160 no.6046 was a powerful loco that was a pleasure to drive and fire, and with a monstrous whistle that could be heard for miles around! Here the loco is seen at Peterborough backing onto its train after running round, as the crew keep a watchful eye for the guard on the platform. *Nathan Wilson*

THOMAS is seen heading away from Yarwell with the British Mk1 coaching set. THOMAS is usually limited to running on the Wansford to Yarwell section only, but does venture to Peterborough on his 'Big Adventure' during the year. *Martin Vos*

THOMAS is seen once again making a spirited departure away from Yarwell, showing the locos versatility by this time hauling the railway's continental rolling stock. THOMAS was initially only fitted with a loco steam brake, but since entering preservation was fitted with both vacuum and air brakes for hauling passenger trains – a really useful engine! *Martin Vos*

The most famous locomotive at the Nene Valley, this plucky little blue tank engine was built in 1947 and has been a Peterborough locomotive all its life. The locomotive worked at the British Sugar Corporation factory in Oundle Road, Peterborough shunting heavy wagons of sugar beet around the factory site and exchange sidings. The loco was replaced by a diesel in the late 1960s and was sold to the Peterborough Railway Society, where it affectionately became known as THOMAS after the Rev. Awdry's character. In 1971, the Rev. Awdry himself attended a PRS open day and officially named the locomotive THOMAS. Here we see THOMAS in a rare move into the carriage and wagon siding to the west of Wansford station, shunting a carriage out of the way ahead of the day's running. *Nathan Wilson*

Another event that THOMAS can be seen at is the Travelling Post Office event. The NVR has two sets of TPO apparatus, located at Yarwell and Sutton Cross. This gives the chance for passengers to witness how the TPO mail exchanges used to take place in days gone by. THOMAS is seen here powering the TPO set towards the apparatus at Sutton Cross prior to exchanging the mail, which can be seen hanging in the large leather pouch. *Martin Vos*

A very busy Wansford yard, with (from L-R) Class 45 Peak no.45041 ROYAL TANK REGIMENT, Hudswell Clarke no.1800 THOMAS, Hunslet Austerity no.75008 SWIFTSURE, Peppercorn A1 Pacific no.60163 TORNADO, Battle of Britain Class no. 34081 92 SQUADRON, Sentinel 0-6-0 diesel shunter DL83 and Deltic no.55022 ROYAL SCOTS GREY all on shed!
Nathan Wilson

Battle of Britain class no.34081 92 SQUADRON coming into steam in readiness for a boiler inspection, while no.3193 NORFOLK REGIMENT prepares to take over passenger duties from Diesel Hydraulic Class 14 no.D9520. *Nathan Wilson*

Left: A class of loco that has seen a variety of members based at the NVR over the years is the 0-6-0 Austerity saddle tank. This one, Hunslet-built no.3193 stands at Wansford water tower topping up its tank under the careful observation of Driver Jennings and Cleaner Rose. This was the locomotive's first day back in public service.
Nathan Wilson

Right: No.3193 NORFOLK REGIMENT has been at the NVR since summer 2019 after completion of a major overhaul. Here the loco is being prepped for a day's service at the NVR, as the early morning mist covers Wansford yard.
Nathan Wilson

A former resident Hunslet Austerity class was WD no.75008 SWIFTSURE. With a light grey haze drifting from the chimney, SWIFTSURE drifts out of Wansford tunnel with a service bound for Yarwell Junction. The locomotive was fitted with air brakes, and the steam powered air pump can be seen on the firemans side of the smokebox. *Nathan Wilson*

With the safety valves feathering, SWIFTSURE stands at Orton Mere awaiting the right away from the guard and to head west towards Overton and Wansford through the Nene Valley. *Nathan Wilson*

A strong and free steaming loco, here no.75008 is seen racing eastwards with a service train for Peterborough, passing Casto
crossing as Driver Nicholson observes the road ahead. *Nathan Wilson*

With a clear exhaust on a warm summer's day, no.75008 SWIFTSURE powers away from Orton Mere around the curve towards Yacht Club crossing with a train for Wansford. *Nathan Wilson*

Above: JACKS GREEN had a sister loco at Nassington of the same class, no.1982 RING HAW which has spent its preservation life working at the North Norfolk Railway after leaving Nassington. In 2015 RING HAW spent the majority of the year operating at NVR, and the opportunity was taken to reunite the two Nassington locos for the first time in over 40 years. Here they are seen together on shed at Wansford. *Nathan Wilson*

Left: The second project for the railway's Small Loco Group is the cosmetic restoration of 16" Hunslet no.1953 JACKS GREEN. The 1939 built loco spent all of its working life at the nearby Nassington Ironstone Quarry a few miles west of Wansford. The loco last ran in the 1980s and had been painted a plain green livery. It is currently being restored to its original livery of green and black with red lining. *Nathan Wilson*

On a grey day, RING HAW is seen on the approach to Mill Lane bridge at Castor with an NVR service train in tow. *Nathan Wilson*

Moving off shed for a day in service, No.1982 RING HAW stands just to the west of Wansford station awaiting the signalman's permission to set back into the station to join the train. Next to the loco is one of the Belgian coaches, carrying the livery of the Wagons Lits 'Orient Express'. The NVR is well known for its use of continental locomotives and rolling stock, due to the track being re-laid to Berne gauge in the early days of preservation. *Nathan Wilson*

Early 2015 saw Hunslet no.1982 RING HAW arrive at the NVR, and for one day ran 'The Nassington Flyer', which was carried by JACKS GREEN when it ran from Nassington to the Peterborough Railway Society's HQ at the sugar beet factory in Peterborough. Here RING HAW is seen on the approach to Castor Crossing from the east. *Nathan Wilson*

At the west end of Wansford tunnel, RING HAW blasts out of the tunnel with a service train to Yarwell Junction. Here the locomotive will run round its train and head east for Peterborough. *Nathan Wilson*

At the 2015 Winter Gala, RING HAW is seen doing what it was designed for – hauling freight. Here the train is seen passing under the A1 road bridge as it heads west towards Yarwell. *Oli Goodman*

The view from the footplate as the countryside rolls past is one of the best views around. Here visiting 16" Hunslet no.1982 RING HAW runs at speed down the Castor straight heading west with a Wansford bound service from Peterborough under clear blue skies. *Nathan Wilson*

Visiting for the 2016 Small Loco event from the North Norfolk Railway, Hudswell Clarke no.1700 WISSINGTON works the local set away from the tunnel towards Yarwell Junction, looking right at home. *Martin Vos*

WISSINGTON is seen passing the Yarwell TPO apparatus with a short freight train, typical of the sort the loco would have hauled in industrial use, at the sugar beet factory on the Wissington Light Railway, which location the loco was named after. *Martin Vos*

One of the highlights of the weekend was reuniting WISSINGTON' with sister loco and NVR resident DEREK CROUCH for the first time in 50 years since they worked together on the Wissington Light Railway. The NVR is also home to an 0-4-0 English Electric diesel shunter named MURIEL which ironically replaced the steam locomotives at Wissington. *Martin Vos*

While on display together, turntable demonstrations were given showing the two locomotives together. A lot of time and effort went into getting WISSINGTON to the NVR and seeing the two together again was a very proud moment for The Small Loco Group. The next time the two locomotives meet, they will both be in steam. *Martin Vos*

At the September steam gala 2014, The Small Loco Group, based at Wansford unveiled their first complete project, the cosmetic restoration of NVR pioneer locomotive Hudswell Clarke saddle tank 0-6-0 no.1539 DEREK CROUCH. Looking through the fireman side cab window of DEREK CROUCH, A1 no.60163 TORNADO can be seen sat on shed at Wansford.
Nathan Wilson

NVR pioneer locos no.1539 DEREK CROUCH and 73050 CITY OF PETERBOROUGH are seen stabled alongside one of the star visitors of the gala, BR Standard 9F no.92212 visiting from the Mid Hants Railway. *Nathan Wilson*

A recreation of what the future holds – smoke drifts from the chimney of DEREK CROUCH as the nameplate catches the light. *Nathan Wilson*

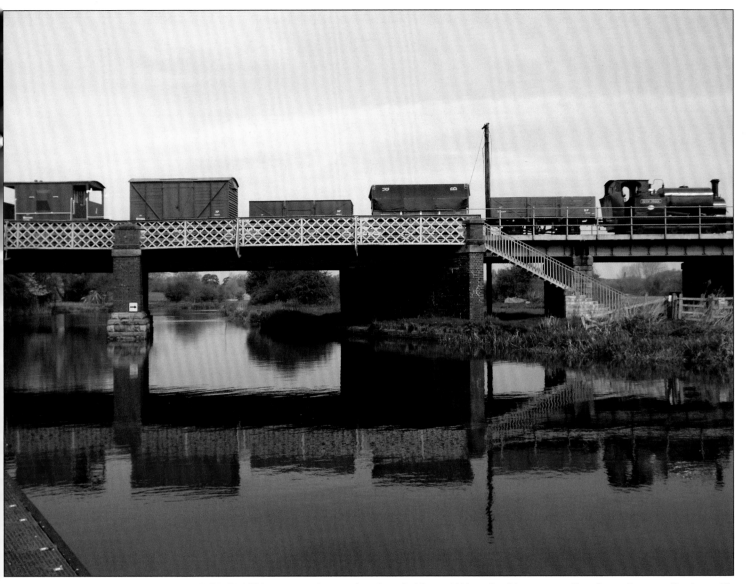

With clear skies overhead, DEREK CROUCH is moved over the river bridge at Wansford in preparation for going on display with the goods train in platform 3 for the railway's inaugural Small Loco Weekend, organised by The Small Loco Group to raise funds for the group and to showcase their work. *Nathan Wilson*

Small locos unite, as visiting Terrier class locomotive no.662 MARTELLO gives brake van rides in Wansford yard at the railway's Southern Winter gala in 2019, passing Hudswell Clarke no.1539 DEREK CROUCH which was being used for turntable demonstrations over the course of the weekend. *Nathan Wilson*

In what could be a photo from the days of British Railways, a freight train stands at Wansford station. The picture was actually taken in 2015 and was taken at the Small Loco Weekend. Scenes like this show what heritage railways are all about. *Nathan Wilson*

This curious looking machine was built by Aveling & Porter, no.9449, and is called BLUE CIRCLE, in recognition of its industrial life working for the Blue Circle cement company. Aveling & Porter are well known for building road locomotives, but did build a handful of railway locomotives, this being the last one they built. BLUE CIRCLE can often be seen giving brake van rides around Wansford. *Nathan Wilson*

OTHER COLOUR ALBUMS!

MAINLINE & MARITIME

PRICES INCLUDE UK P&P

OPERATING HERITAGE DIESELS
On the footplate with the Diesel Department on the Spa Valley Railway
by Tim Wood

£16.95

Featuring Classes 09, 10, 12, 14, 17, 20, 25, 26, 27, 31, 33, 37, 42, 50, 55, 73 and more!

THE GWILI AT 40
Wales' First Standard Gauge Heritage Railway
by Iain McCall

£12.95

GWR Branch Lines Today No. 1

BEHIND THE SCENES ON THE NORTH YORKSHIRE MOORS RAILWAY

£17.95

by Andrew Jeffery

NIGHT TRAINS OF BRITISH RAIL

£18.95

Alan Whitehouse

WORLD STEAM IN FOCUS ALBUM NO. 1

£17.95

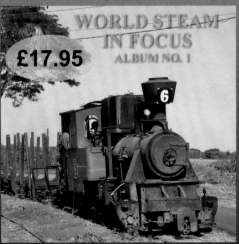

From the publishers of LOCOMOTIVES INTERNATIONAL magazine

BY POST: 3 Broadleaze, Upper Seagry, near Chippenham, SN15 5EY
BY PHONE: (+44) 01275 845012 (24 hr answerphone)
ORDER ONLINE AT: www.mainlineandmaritime.co.uk
BY EMAIL / PAYPAL: iain@mainlineandmaritime.co.uk

LOCOMOTIVES
INTERNATIONAL

THE MAGAZINE FOR FANS OF INTERNATIONAL RAILWAYS!

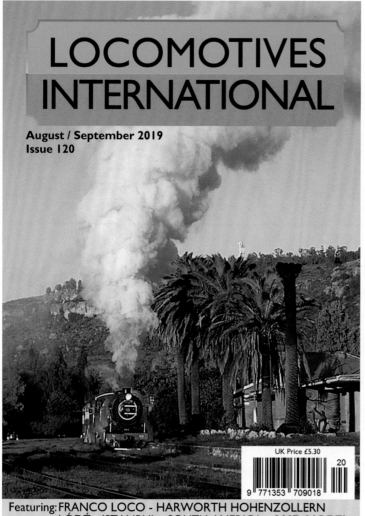

LOCOMOTIVES
INTERNATIONAL

August / September 2019
Issue 120

UK Price £5.30

9 771353 709018   20

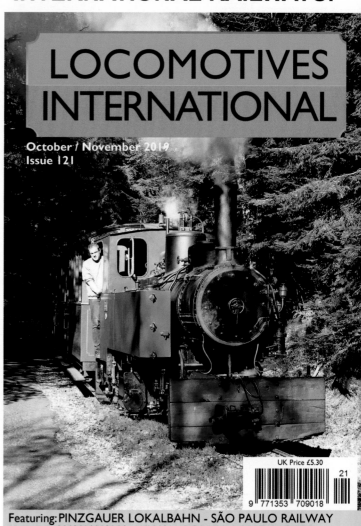

LOCOMOTIVES
INTERNATIONAL

October / November 2019
Issue 121

UK Price £5.30

9 771353 709018   21

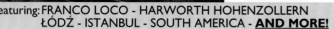

Featuring: FRANCO LOCO - HARWORTH HOHENZOLLERN
ŁÓDŹ - ISTANBUL - SOUTH AMERICA - **AND MORE!**

Featuring: PINZGAUER LOKALBAHN - SÃO PAULO RAILWAY
WAKAYAMA - KWAI - BOLIVIA - **AND MORE!**